C000274278

LOVE
LOVE ME

♥

*To be brave is to love
someone unconditionally,
without expecting
anything in return.
To just give ...*

LOVE

LOVE ME

MARIANNE VICELICH

This hardback edition published in December 2011

National Library of Australia
Cataloguing-in-Publication entry
Author: Vicelich, Marianne
Title: Love. Love Me/Marianne Vicelich
ISBN: 978-0-646-56803-4 (hbk.)

Design Di Quick
Printed and bound in China
through Haha Printing
Published by Seaview Press, Australia

Other books by Marianne Vicelich

Bat Your Eyelashes.
How To Be Well Mannered With Style.
Published 2008

The Glossy Life.
How To Be Glamorously Economic.
Published 2009

♥

CONTENTS

CONTENTS

LOVE, LOVE, LOVE YOURSELF

♥

For attractive lips,
speak words of kindness.

For lovely eyes,
seek out the good in people.

For a slim figure,
share your food with the hungry.

For beautiful hair,
let a child run his or her fingers
through it once a day.

For poise,
walk with the knowledge you
will never walk alone.

We leave you a tradition
with a future.

The tender loving care of
human beings
will never become obsolete.

♥

People even more than things
have to be restored,
renewed, revived, reclaimed,
redeemed, redeemed and redeemed.
Never throw out anybody.

Remember,
if you need a helping hand,
you'll find one at the end
of your arm.

As you grow older,
you will discover
that you have two hands;
one for helping yourself,
the other for helping others.

The beauty of a woman
is not in the clothes she wears,
the figure that she carries,
or the way she combs her hair.
The beauty of a woman
must be seen from in her eyes,
because that is the
doorway to her heart,
the place where love resides.

The beauty of a woman
is not in a facial mole,
but true beauty in a woman
is reflected in her soul.

It is the caring that she
lovingly gives,
the passion that she knows.

And the beauty of a woman,
with passing years will only grow!

1973 SAM LEVENSON
(THIS POEM WAS LOVED AND OFTEN
QUOTED BY AUDREY HEPBURN)

*To love oneself
is the beginning
of a lifelong
romance ...*

Accept who you are. Virginia Woolf wrote,
"One of the signs of passing youth is the birth
of a sense of fellowship with other human
beings as we take our place among them.
And a sense of fellowship with oneself. I am
not so hard on me anymore. I am no longer
constantly criticising, and no longer seeing the
body as merely a catalogue of imperfections
– but as a catalogue of womanliness."

When I loved myself enough
I quit settling for too little and I began
to see I didn't have to chase after life.
If I am quiet and hold still,
life comes to me.
Desires of the heart do come
when you love yourself.
I quit exhausting myself by trying so hard.
I began to feel a community within.
This inner team with diverse talents and
idiosyncrasies is my strength and my potential.
I became my own authority by listening
to the wisdom of my heart.

When I loved myself enough I saw that
what I resisted persisted like a small child
tugging my skirt. Now I am curious and
gentle when resistance comes tugging.

♥

*"Happiness depends
upon ourselves"*

ARISTOTLE

To always remember ...

*That a life driven by love
is preferable to a
life driven by greed or ambition.*

*That it is amazing
how much support you get when
you tell the truth.*

*That desire is a much more
robust concept than we
sometimes give it credit for.*

*That it is wise to
distance yourself from people
who want to flatten you.*

*That there is not a person
alive who doesn't want to be
told that they are loved.*

Take a deep breath.
Think of three things
to be thankful for.
Let the gratitude flow
through you ...
smile.

"Often we don't even realise who we're meant to be because we're so busy trying to live out someone else's ideas.

But other people and their opinions hold no power in defining our destiny."

OPRAH WINFREY, O MAGAZINE,
NOVEMBER 2009

If you are comfortable
in your own skin,
you allow others
to be comfortable in theirs.
Don't compare yourself
to someone else.

Value yourself
and your career.

Carl Jung and Aristotle ... on love

Carl Jung believed that your life needs
meaning and purpose if you are to be happy.
He refers to this as a spiritual quest,
a dream quest or a major passion.
Having a passion raises your self-esteem.
You are less focused on whether or
not you look perfect on the outside,
when you feel amazing on the inside.

Self-love is essential if you are to love
and be loved by another. Aristotle believed
it to be the very first condition to achieve
the highest form of love - a relationship of
shared virtue. Without self-love, Aristotle
purported that a human was not able to extend
sympathy and affection. Aristotle also didn't
feel that self-love was hedonistic or egotistic.
Aristotle felt self-love was a reflection of
your pursuit of the noble and virtuous.

PASSION TAKES YOU PLACES

♥

"*Life can be a rocky road.*
The challenge is not
to let it grind you into
dust, but to polish you
into a brilliant gem."

JOHN MILTON FOGG

♥

*Passion
takes you
places* ...

Accomplishments makes us happy.
Never underestimate the power
that lies in work.

Build confidence by completing
tasks you set out to do.

Treat yourself with dignity
and appreciation.

Be assured that you are
a highly capable individual.

Let go.

*Express gratitude for all that you
have been blessed with.*

*Take a proactive action that is
beneficial for you everyday.*

*Get off your anger/fear treadmill.
Nourish your inner strength and enhance
the overall quality of your life by reducing
anger and fear related stress.*

*Define daily personal goals and sustain
the effort to achieve them.*

*Use positive self-talk to re-frame
your mood in a positive light.*

*Expand your vision.
Think of five things that are
interesting to you, then make the
decision to start engaging
in them.*

♥

In life the lows will pass.
They come into our life for a reason –
to enrich us, to draw us closer into the
vast, glittery vividness of what it is to be human.
Pain softens our hard edges and deepens
our interaction with others.
Pain is like that tree being pruned
to make it grow strong.
And beautiful.

It helps us learn so that we can then
venture into the world wiser, softer,
richer more compassionate.
It is all part of a bigger picture,
a scarred, complex, intricate,
glorious map of our living.

Lead a full life.
Have lots to do.
Meet people.
Engage in interesting fun activities.
Love your work.
Go to the cinema ...
turn up to an activity ...
eat a meal out
... alone.
Go on holiday solo.

Mastering the art of being busy
and independently active
is the key.

Poet Gregory Corso wrote
that standing on a street corner
waiting for no-one is power,
and it is absolutely without
question the truth.

The ingredients
for self-love ...

You must show self-love for your soul –
in pursuing your passions, your soul will be
stimulated allowing personal growth to happen.

Show self-love for your body – by treating
your body well and loving it – imperfections
and all. If you are feeling insecure about your
body, build up your self-esteem by exercising
regularly and having a healthy diet. If you are
doing everything in your control to achieve your
highest potential, you will feel more confident.

Forgive yourself for not being perfect by keeping
in mind this story about Coco Chanel. When
Coco accidentally singed her hair, instead of
feeling insecure and unattractive about her new
hair she boldly chopped off her hair even more.
Coco then proudly went to the opera with a new
short tomboyish hairstyle. She had started a new
fashion trend. The next day, women began visiting
their hair salons, requesting Coco's hairstyle ...

Love love me

Calm is impossible
if you want to
control other people,
for their will is
like an eel, always slipping
from your grasp.
Let go.

♥

*Impulsive behaviour is often
not the best behaviour.*

*Thoughtful action
is always preferable
because it gives the leeway
to find a better way forward.*

*Take a deep breath and let the
right choice come to you.*

*Listen to your inner voice –
it is always seeking goodness,
happiness and peace
for you.*

Resistance is so draining.

There is a beauty to gracious acceptance,
an energy that leads to peace.

In a vexing situation try laughing
rather than snarling, try combating
with a light heart.

You will ultimately be the winner –
for you will have the gift of serenity.

Try letting go of the situation you
cannot control, the one that's sapping
your energy and churning your sleep.

Flood your life with the relief of
walking away, with dignity.

*Live with
confidence and joy.
There is so much
wonder and beauty
in this world.
Seek it.*

TRUST YOURSELF

♥

Love love me

♥

*Trust your inner voice
it might just
save your life …*

"If you are strong,
your character will speak for itself.
If you are weak,
words will be of no help."

JOHN F KENNEDY,
FROM AN ADDRESS HE WAS TO DELIVER
ON NOVEMBER 22, 1963.

Learn to grieve
for the hurts in life
when they happen instead
of making your heart heavy
from lugging them around.

Forgive yourself
for all the times you
thought you were
not good enough.

Listen to the wisdom
of your body,
it speaks so clearly
through its fatigue,
sensitivities, aversions
and hungers.

Quit
fearing your fear.

Quit
rehashing the past and
worrying about the future.

Keep in the present
where aliveness lives.

Realise that your mind
can torment and deceive you,
but in the service of your heart,
it is a great and noble ally.

Try not to get caught
in the abyss of emotions,
because emotions ebb and flow.
You can't hold onto a raft of sadness always,
eventually that emotion will go out to
sea and you won't always be sad.
Pessimists take things personally,
and believe that their situation is
permanent and that problems are pervasive.
Optimists are the opposite as they
understand that things change.
They believe that their situation is
transient and it will pass.
Both happiness and sadness are
not lasting.

Use your anger for something positive
and good. Don't let a situation be
complicated by your negativity.

Don't be afraid of sharing your vulnerabilities
— your fear, envy, frustration. It will make
you realise that you are not alone as your
vulnerabilities are shared by many.

William James, the philosopher,
wrote about how he viewed the world
as having two kinds of people:
Once-Born and Twice-Born.

James described Once-Born
people as never wandering too far from
the safety of who they thought they were.
When a crisis arrived,
pushing them to enter into dark places
where they might find hidden parts of
themselves, they never bothered to flip
those self-illumination switches.
They chose instead to remain
sitting in the dark.

In contrast,
Twice-Born people used a shake-up
in their outer world as an opportunity to wake up
their inner world – seeking a more profound view
on life – and their purpose and potential in it.
Twice-Born people viewed a crisis as an
initiation by fire into a more conscious,
more fulfilling way of living.

I have always loved James'
definition of Twice-Born people.
After every challenge in my life,
I have always consciously chosen to be
determined to be re-born into someone
wiser, stronger, and happier.

*Believe in this better future
and it will help you
stay on path to finding it.*

Love love me

"Never look back
unless you're planning
to go that way."

HENRY DAVID THOREAU

The transformative effect of keeping a journal ...

If you're going through a challenging time
right now, buy a journal, and begin writing
about how you may envision your unexpected
path will lead you to a new and better path.

Writing in a journal can be a great way to release
energy and patch the soul when it is wounded.
It is a great creative resource as well. What you
write – be it the details of your personal life,
concepts or snippets and stories from your day –
is up to you. A journal can be a great way to let
off some steam or deal with pent-up energies.

A journal is a particularly effective means to
delve into feelings. It is a place to have a one-way
conversation about anything you like. You can
express feelings, ideas or fears there without ever
having to worry about what someone will say. For
the time you are writing in the journal, it is all
about what you are feeling in a secure and
safe environment.

Kindness ...

Kindness is an indispensable virtue
from which most of the other virtues flow,
the wellspring of our happiness.
It assumes and does not demand
that others will reciprocate and is in that
way determinedly optimistic. Kindness
shelters a variety of highly valued traits
– empathy, generosity, unselfishness,
tolerance, acceptance, and compassion.

Courage ...

The essence of courage
is overcoming fear.
The ability to sustain the inevitable
disappointments that life deals
each of us and respond with a determination
not to be defeated is one of the
highest forms of courage.

Dependability ...

At a personal level,
fidelity and dependability are
indispensable to the intimacy we all seek.
We cannot be close to anyone on whose
words we cannot depend and whose
promises we cannot believe.

———✦———

*"As we let our own light shine,
we unconsciously give other people
permission to do the same"*

NELSON MANDELA

THE WORD IS LOVE

♥

Years ago in New York
I ran into a cathedral
to escape a sudden thunderstorm.
A priest, mid-sermon,
was saying that
at the end of our lives
the question should be
not what we have done,
but how well we have loved.
The older I get
the more I respect kindness
and generosity of spirit.
There are only two ways to live
– the victim or the fighter.
The fighter of courage and grace.

♥

We can crack open
our life to love by the
simple action of giving it.
Being loving invites
love to us.

"A woman gains worth when
she lives how she wishes to live.
To be happy with her choices.
To have the freedom to make
her own decisions.
To be independent and autonomous.
To be proud of her challenges
and achievements —
emotional and professional."

ELENA FOSTER,
EDUCATOR, SPAIN

Self esteem ...

The concept of self-esteem dovetails
into multiple facets of you. It is connected
to your sense of worth and feelings of efficacy,
and it pertains to a personal evaluation of yourself.
In an ideal world,
you would hold a very high opinion of yourself,
which you would use to establish your core or
set point – the rules or schemas you use
to navigate your life.
Unfortunately, this is not always the
case, as you may look externally for validation or to
gain perspective on where you stand in life, relying
on these external opinions and
views as a measure of your
own self worth.

While most of us would assert that we
were raised to believe that our inner
worth is inviolate and intrinsic, when life
pitches us a curveball, doubts can mess
up our game and shake our resolve.

♥

Criticism is merely a report
from another person that points out
disapproval with respect to some action,
opinion, or behaviour, in other words,
it shouldn't be a frightening prospect.
One of the seminal features of cognitive behaviour
therapy is the stubborn refusal to buy in to
an individual's sense of worthlessness.
Take a look at what your internal editor
says when you face criticism and
pressure from others to conform,
or even worse when you berate yourself.
Develop a new script.

If you still insist you are not worthy
make a list of your supposed worthiness
to try to prove it to yourself. Do the maths.
In short you will discover that the so-called hard
evidence you present to yourself to back
up your "worthless theory"
will be nonsense.

Fight the negative messages
you are so often exposed to and
build up your self-esteem.

Learn from criticism. If you feel that what
you are hearing is constructive, heed it.
If you think it is cruel disregard it.

Release, relax, and remember these
words can only hurt you if you let them.
Your self-worth does not depend upon
someone else's opinion of you.

Self-worth cannot solely be built through
what you do. Of course achievements can
bring you satisfaction, but they are not
autonomously responsible for true happiness.

These affirmations
will help to empower you
even in difficult times ....

I respect myself for who I am,
not merely for what I do

I have skills and attributes,
talents and passions

I have ambitions, I know that
I can achieve what I set out to do

I am kind and honest,
and I believe in the good in life

I appreciate my body and
feel happy to be alive.
I treat myself well,
and I pray for strength
and compassion

I am worthy,
valid and a worthwhile
individual

Confidence Tricks

Insecurity can arise when we face challenges,
and we compound this with unrealistic
goals and negative self-talk.
Confidence is like a muscle – it needs
to be used, or it weakens.

"Eat the elephant one bite at a time,"
goes the proverb. When faced with a
daunting project, divide it into manageable
pieces and do one at a time.
When you finish, move onto the next step.

Humans naturally tend towards self-doubt.
The mind is continually telling some version
of the "I can't do it" story, so don't assume
it will be helpful. A better approach is to
acknowledge the self-limiting thought,
but continue to practise what you
need to do, over and over again.
Acting confident comes first,
feeling confident comes later.

Lack of confidence is
a habit that has been created
in response to situations,
and it is underpinned by fear —
perhaps of failure, embarrassment,
or disappointment — which may
have been buried for years.
Each time we face our fear we gain
strength, courage, and confidence.
Feel the fear, smile,
and say, gently but firmly,
'I see you, I accept you,
but I am moving forward.'

Once you get the rhythm of positive
thoughts about yourself you can
accomplish almost anything.

Somewhere in your childhood,
your well-meaning parents passed on
feelings of insecurity and displayed
feelings of inadequacy and fear.
At that point, you began to deny
your own magnificence.

♥

These thoughts and feelings
were never true, and they
certainly are not true now.
As children, we received
most of our negative
messages from adults.

Today,
when most of us look in the mirror,
we will say something negative.
To look yourself in the eye and make
a positive declaration is one of the
quickest ways to get a positive
result with affirmations.

Events come and go,
but the love you have
for yourself can be constant,
and it is the most important
quality you possess in life.
If something wonderful happens,
go to the mirror and say "thank you."
Acknowledge yourself for creating
this wonderful experience.

Love is never
outside yourself –
it's always within you.
As you are more loving
you will be more
lovable.

CHAPTER 5

REACH
FOR
YOUR DREAMS

♥

*Do something each day to bring you
a little closer to your dreams.*

*"All the strength you need to achieve
anything is within you. Don't wait for a
light to appear at the end of the tunnel, stride
down there ... and light it yourself."*

SARA HENDERSON

Seeding is believing.
If you are seeding positive thoughts
and positive habits, then success will eventually
blossom. If you're starting to feel itchy and twitchy
because change is not happening as speedily as
you want, envisage what you want on a delivery
truck coming towards you, it's just a bit stuck in
traffic but coming towards you right now.
The universe's delays are not
necessarily the universe's
denials.

Ban the words
"always" and "never"
from your vocabulary.
Become aware of using
too much "pervasiveness"
and "permanence"
in your stories.

*Affirmations to help
empower you to reach
for your dreams ...*

Wisdom
I dismantle the power struggle
and find my balance

Optimism
I am productive,
capable and intelligent

Responsibility
I retain my individuality.
I actualise my abilities

Tenacity
I choose harmony.
I find the balance in my life

Honesty
I share my feelings.
I am able to build trust

THE DECISION TO TAKE CONTROL

♥

"Perhaps the gravest injustice
faced in the whole world
is the one faced by women.
For centuries we have been denied our worth,
particularly the value placed on us by
our families, societies, countries and
the universe.
Every culture I know has its own
sets of unjust views, practices,
and laws toward women.
When it comes to the value of our worth,
the global south and the north
are equally guilty in their marginalisation
of our issues and voice,
even if the degrees differ in its extremity."

"Yet we talk about a world that
needs more peace than wars in it,
more prosperity than poverty,
more health than sickness,
more happiness than sadness,
and more beauty than cruelty;
humanity simply cannot attain
such goals without the full

♥

acknowledgement of women's worth,
or without the full inclusion
of women in all decision-making powers,
from the family to the higher authority
of the government, of religious and
of economic institutions.
Perhaps humanity's biggest act of injustice
toward itself is by denying and silencing
half of its population and the
other half of its knowledge,
the sacred feminine.

A woman's worth is in the wisdom she brings,
the strength she has, the beauty she carries,
the kindness she shows, the courage she lives,
and the patience she practices.
The world needs women so it may sustain itself.
It is time to give women
the acknowledgment and recognition
of their values for justice
and for a better world."

ZAINAB SALBI,
FOUNDER AND CEO, WOMEN FOR
WOMEN INTERNATIONAL, IRAQ

When you have faith
in your abilities
and accept who you are,
you will uncover your unique gifts ...

Be responsible for yourself.

Work at being
a whole human being.

Being able to validate yourself,
honestly confront yourself and soothe
yourself in difficult moments.

Be a grown-up
running your own life.

Be your own best friend.
Honour your goals,
challenges and dreams.

Notice the positive.
Foster the positive by
focusing on what's good.

Make an effort
to do little things for people.
Small things count.

A small compliment,
a loving touch,
a little gift,
these all feed the
wellbeing of others.

Express affection
regularly and generously.

Respect everyone's opinions
instead of being dogmatic
about your own.

Listen and compromise
in any given situation.

Don't be afraid of conflict.
Be honest
even about difficult issues.

It is okay if disagreements arise
as it's the way you deal with them
that makes all the difference.

Make time for fun and humour.

Celebrate love
in your idiosyncratic way.

The aim is to manage your life rather
than simply let it happen to you.
So much unhappiness
stems from a lack of control.
You shape your life, no-one else.

Change your pattern of thinking now.
There is a well-known saying
attributed to Abraham Lincoln that
"people are usually about as happy
as they make up their
minds to be."

BE
YOUR OWN
PERSON

♥

*"Happiness
is the meaning
and the purpose of life,
the whole aim and end
of human existence"*

ARISTOTLE

You can never create love in your
life by talking or thinking about being lonely.
Feeling lonely or needy just pushes people
away. The first relationship to improve
is the one you have with yourself.
When you are happy with yourself,
then all your other relationships improve too.
A happy person is very attractive to others.
If you are looking for more love,
then you need to love yourself more.
When you are needy for love,
it means that you are missing love
and approval from the most important
person you know and that's you.

Pamper yourself.
Buy yourself flowers for your home
and surround yourself with everything
that pleases you. Life always mirrors
back to us the feelings we have inside.
When you are able to contribute to the
fulfillment of your own needs, then
you won't be so needy and
co-independent.

Autonomy

The *Journal of Personality
and Social Psychology* nominated "autonomy",
defined as "the feeling that your life, its activities
and habits, are self-chosen and self-endorsed",
as important to achieving happiness.
Having a strong sense of control of one's life,
autonomy, is a more dependable predictor of
positive feelings of well-being than any of the
objective conditions of life and self-worth.

Independence

There are many joys and advantages of being
unattached – imagine how great it would be if you
could also enjoy most of these in a relationship.
After a break-up of any kind of partnership, it
is especially good to have a spell by yourself.
It can be tough, but it is certainly better than
rushing, with all your emotional neediness,
straight into a new relationship. Look around
you, happy singles make happy couples.

Letter to
Zsa-Zsar Gabor

"Dear Zsa-Zsar,
I'm breaking off my engagement
to a very wealthy man.
He gave me a beautiful house,
a mink coat,
diamonds,
a stove and
an expensive car.
What shall I do?"

ZSAR-ZSAR GABOR
"SEND BACK THE STOVE."

♥

America's former Secretary of State,
Madeleine Albright,
was once regarded as one of
the world's most powerful women.
This is what she said about being a wife,
"In the twenty – three years
that I was married to Joe,
his tastes became mine.
After he left,
I rediscovered the fact
that I did not like beef –
even though for years we had
eaten it almost every night."
Ah, so even Madame Secretary –
entrusted with the foreign policy of one
of the world's strongest nations
– has known, in her private life,
the creep of capitulation,
how much a woman's
most basic choices can be
reoriented by her partner.

Keep your independence and
autonomy no matter what.

WAKE UP SLEEPY MINDS, HEARTS AND SPIRITS

♥

Women are magnetic beings.
Which means that things come to us,
always. The only reason we chase anything
is when we don't believe in ourselves
or are unaware of our power.

"Twenty years from now
you will be more disappointed
by the things you didn't do
than by the ones you did do.
So throw off the bowlines.
Sail away from safe harbour.
Catch the trade winds in your sails.
Explore. Dream. Discover."

MARK TWAIN

Begin each day
with saying thank you
for three things,
no matter how large or
small they are.
Gratitude leads to
contentment,
which leads to joy.
And joy is a most effective
medicine.

---

*Try and look
gorgeous
in some way
everyday.
Life is too
fleeting
not to.*

Surrender can require
just as much strength
as resistance.
It brings relief and freedom
and enlightenment.
And often the higher ground,
with the grace of it.

Treat your enemy
like your best friend.
Stun them,
soften their heart.

Never forget
the power of forgiveness.
It can be incredibly releasing
– it can flush you clean,
uplift you,
move you on.

꧁

A life lived in fear
is a life not fully lived.

Live with gratitude,
entwined with your goodness.

What nourishes the soul
– silence, emptiness,
laughter, and nature.
A child's joy.
Rest.

*" It is never
too late to be
what you might
have been".*

GEORGE ELLIOT

"*I'm not going
to lie down and let
trouble walk over me*"

ELLEN GLASGOW

Creativity nourishes us;
it brings us
exhilaration and solace.
We all need
to nurture our creativity
– it's soul food.

Simplify any problem or obstacle ...

The children's show Sesame Street
has an ongoing concept
called Twinkle Think.
It shows 3 little cutesy fairies
having a problem
– then they Twinkle Think –
by stopping their state of panic to pause,
relax and together come up
with a solution.
If you have a problem today,
take a moment to "Twinkle Think."
As Einstein reminds us,
you can't solve a problem at the
same energy it is created.

TANTALISING THE MIND

♥

"…. *cheerfulness
and content
are great beautifiers,
and are famous preservers
of youthful looks.*"

CHARLES DICKENS

*Tantalising
the mind ...*

For mindful breathing ...

Sit for 10 minutes per day.
Focus on your breathing, sit comfortably
with your hands on your lap and close your eyes.
Put your hands on your belly to feel
the rise and fall of your breath.
Be prepared for distractions and
fidgeting.

For mindful listening ...

Gather together household items
such as pencils, paper, coins, a pot.
Place them in a box and close your
eyes, then focus on the individual
sounds you make with them.

Love love me

♥

For mindful seeing ...

Go into a park.
Close your eyes and write in a gratitude
journal descriptions of what you can see.

For mindful smelling ...

Smell four very different items.
For example, peanut butter, a rose,
a cinnamon stick and mint.
Write down what they remind you of.

For mindful tasting ...

When you eat be aware of the flavours
and taste sensations of various foods.

For mindful movement ...

Turn on the radio and dance.

The art of playing

Ask a child if they would like to play a game and you will see their eyes light up, but ask a grown up and you will probably see a look of surprise, uncertainty and doubt.

As experts have noted too many adults have forgotten the value of play. For a child, play is the essential tool for learning about life, a bridge to reality. Through play, a child experiments with different ways of constructing the world, for organising feelings and thoughts, and making sense of the complexities of social interaction.

For an adult, it offers access to the unconscious processes within. And in science, imaginative play stimulates creative insight and discovery. In games, children learn how to get along with one another, and in may tribal communities, games continue to serve as a means of developing

relational skills. They may even decide the
political and economic future of a nation.
Games show astronauts how to dock in space,
and they are even used — for better or worse —
to predict the outcome of thermonuclear war.

At home, a casual game of cards may
help us unwind, while a recreational game
like tennis can enhance our health.
Complex games like chess can help
us improve our concentration and cognitive
skills, and if they are carefully concentrated,
they can even help us to achieve a
state of mind that brings us into
extraordinary states of consciousness
and peak performance. In such a state,
we are functioning at our best.

If games are so potent in developing childhood,
adult, and therapeutic skills, why not employ
them for the development of love. If we
approached relationships as we would a
complex game — with dedication, imagination,
and a willingness to learn, we could, bring
deeper meaning and enjoyment to our lives.

♥

"*Imagination
is more important
than knowledge,
for knowledge is limited,
while imagination
embraces the entire
world.*"

ALBERT EINSTEIN

LOVE YOUR BODY

♥

Love love me

♥

"In the midst
of winter,
I found there was,
within me,
an invinsible
summer."

ALBERT CAMUS

Love your body

Your entire body ... muscle, bone,
brain tissue, blood vessels, red blood cells,
hormones and enzymes ... just about every
squiggle of you ... needs protein everyday
to renew itself and go on living.
The nutritionists say you also
need minerals, vitamins, a little fat,
and carbohydrates (natural ones like
the sugars and starch in fresh fruits).
If you starve your body long enough
for vital supplies, you can develop
a severe vitamin mineral or
protein deficiency.

If you want to keep your soul alive to
accomplish your goals, you have to keep
your body well-nourished and hydrated.
You can start by eating lots of fish.
In fact, Dr. Joseph R. Hibbeln
performed a study which showed

that high fish-eating countries like
Japan and Taiwan have very
low rates of depression,
while low fish-eating countries like
Germany and the U.S. have high rates.
Indeed, overall, major depression is 60 times more
prevalent in countries where little fish is eaten.

Preferably eat your fish in a
"supercharged meal" – which means
having your healthy fish, with
carbohydrates (brown rice), and
some greens (salad or spinach).
Plus research shows that there is a
10% decrease in your mental performance when
you feel thirsty. Meaning, you should also drink
beverage products that support rapid hydration
and contain all the essential electrolytes.

Try to get at least 51 grams of protein
into you every day. More would be better
but try for at least 17 grams a meal.
Here are approximate protein values you will
need a big helping of one of these at every meal.

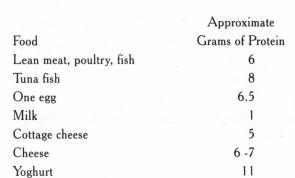

Food	Approximate Grams of Protein
Lean meat, poultry, fish	6
Tuna fish	8
One egg	6.5
Milk	1
Cottage cheese	5
Cheese	6 -7
Yoghurt	11

After protein fill up with fresh fruit,
raw or lightly cooked vegetables,
and whole-grain breads.

Nibble on raw carrots,
a few peanuts or walnuts in the shell,
celery stalks,
an apple, an orange.

Go for the high powered
vitamins and minerals.

Drink this body cocktail daily –
Put into a blender ¹/₂ cup pineapple,
2 tablespoons soybean oil,
1 teaspoon calcium lactate,
1 teaspoon vanilla and 1 cup milk.
Start blender and
add ¹/₂ cup powdered skim milk,
and ¹/₂ tablespoon brewer's yeast
or dried liver powder.
When well blended,
add mixture to remainder of milk.
Banana, orange juice, berries or other fruit
may be used instead of pineapple.
Gradually increase the yeast or liver powder
from ¹/₂ tablespoon to 1–2 tablespoons.
Drink this daily …

Fresh fruit is best.
Buy fresh fruits and fresh vegetables
even when cooking just for yourself.

Cook with a light touch,
to the point of having things almost
underdone, meat too. Use less water for
vegetables than recipes call for and then
drain it off in a glass and drink it yourself.
That is where all the vitamins are.

Make these substitutions in cooking.
Use stone ground whole wheat, soy
instead of white. Use spinach, artichoke or
whole-wheat noodles instead of
starchy white ones.
Use brown sugar instead of white.
Make salad dressings and sauté food
with soybean oil exclusively.
Soybean oil has tremendous amounts
of polyunsaturated fatty acids which
every cell of your body cries for.
Buy unsalted butter.

You almost can't get too much protein.
The excess you acquire over your
daily requirements helps you
burn extra fat.

Walk everywhere

Why this works ...

Walk when you might drive or take a taxi.
Research shows that 60 to 90 minutes of walking
a day is needed to maintain body weight.
That may sound a lot, but if you are doing
it in 10 to 15–minute increments,
you won't notice it.

Cycle

Why it works ...

Even moderate cycling uses more calories than
driving and a study in the *American Journal
of Public Health* concluded that more than
half the difference in obesity rates among
countries is linked to walking and
cycling habits.

Drink black coffee instead of a milky latte

Why it works ...

Black coffee has zero calories.
A large latte can contain up to 200
calories, and that's without sugar.

Eat three meals a day

Why it works ...

While dieters are sometimes encouraged to
eat five to six small meals a day, this is not
backed by strong scientific evidence.
Encouraging people to eat five or six times
a day when they are not hungry alienates
them from crucial body signals that can
help them lose weight naturally.

Love Dogs

Why it works ...
In France, dogs are allowed on public transport
and welcomed in holiday accommodation.
The French take them everywhere which means
they exercise consistently, a key to weight loss.
Researchers have found that dog owners
are less likely to skip exercise than gym
members. What's more, studies show the
average dog owner exercises their dog twice
a day for 24 minutes each time and takes
their dog out on three long walks each week
– that's more than eight hours of walking.

Eat at the table

Why it works ...
Research shows that eating a meal slowly,
over 30 minutes resting your cutlery between
bites and chatting, leads to a greater
concentration of satiety hormones,
which stops you over-eating.

CHAPTER 11

WELLBEING

♥

Caring
for Your
Emotional
Self

Write down what you loved
to do in childhood.
Chances are you will still enjoy
those things and can incorporate
them into your life now.

Sing your heart out.
You can always find a few spare minutes.
Use that time to play some music.
The Institute of Music,
Health and Education
has found that just 5 minutes
of singing or humming can put
you in a sunnier mood.

♥

Levity – humour, lightness, laughter.
Nurture these aspects of living for
anti-aging effects and good health.
The neuroscientist Lee Berk
says laughter can make you healthier.
It can lower blood pressure,
cut stress hormone levels,
reduce pain, relax muscles,
boost immunity and pump you
full of endorphins.

Surround yourself with light.
In addition to light-hearted people,
surround yourself with lighter images.
Take a vacation from the news and
get rid of visual negativity.

Calming the mind

Stress has become
such a big factor among women.
We have grown accustomed to a
certain level of it in our lives.
It is sort of like a low grade
flu we walk around with.
According to one theory, even when
there is nothing currently worthy
of our anxiety, we may fret
over a minor issue simply
because our low-grade stress
needs someplace to go.
We have what some experts
call "stress seekers."

It is no fun to live in a state of
heightened stress, but beyond the
bad feeling, it can lead to multiple
health problems such as headaches,
stomach problems, lowered immunity,
colds, even perhaps infertility.

When you act really stressed,
running around annoyed or like
a rattled snake, looking as if you
could come unglued at any moment,
you give away your power.
To other people, you seem out of
control, unfocused, even unreliable.

There is no cure for stress,
you have to attack it from different angles.
The starting point is
to develop lifestyle habits that
make your body feel better able to
endure those slings and arrows
of outrageous fortune.
If you eat right, exercise regularly,
get enough sleep, you are going to
feel less prone to physical manifestations
of anxiety. But no matter how great
shape you are in, there will be moments
when you feel like flipping out.

To help ....

Experiment until you find
an instant de-stresser that helps
you calm down quickly in a bad situation.
Maybe it is something as basic as counting
to ten or taking three deep breaths.
Or maybe it's repeating
a calming mantra to yourself.
Running your fingers lightly
along the underside of your arm between
the wrist and elbow is amazingly relaxing.
An instant de-stresser is not going to
have miraculous results,
but it buys you time and lets you
think with a clearer head.

Resist the urge to "awfulise."
Women have a tendency to imagine the worst.
You have to train yourself not to jump
too far ahead, or at least be able to play
out positive scenarios in your head.
Tell yourself you are only going to react to the
news at hand and not skip ahead too far.

Go into fact-finding mode.
Stress is often heightened because there
is an unknown element to the situation –
and the unknown can be very scary.
Do not jump ahead and awfulise.
Full knowledge both gives you a wonderful
sense of control and relieves your anxiety.

Create a secret soother,
something you do on a regular basis
that brings you a sense of bliss.
This is not something you could
save until things get crazy.
This should be a pleasurable,
calming activity you engage in on
a regular basis because it keeps your
stress set point as low as possible.
Whatever you decide on,
keep it as your secret.
For whatever your reason,
soothers seem even better
when you have them all to
yourself …

*This one
is a keeper ...
by an unknown
author ...*

"By the time the Lord made women,
he was into his sixth day of working overtime.
An angel appeared and asked, "Why are you
spending so much time on this one?" And the
Lord answered, "Have you seen my spec sheet
on her? She has to be completely washable but
not plastic; have over 200 movable parts, all
replaceable; be able to run on Diet Coke and
leftovers; have a lap that can hold four children
at a time; have a kiss that can cure anything
from a scraped knee to a broken heart –
and she has to do everything
with only two hands."

The angel was astounded at the requirements.
"Only two hands?! No way! And that's just
on the standard model? That's too much work
for one day. Wait until tomorrow to finish."

"But I won't," the Lord protested.
"I'm so close to finishing this creation that's so
close to my own heart ... she already heals herself
when she's sick, and she can work 18-hour days."
The angel moved closer and touched the woman.
"But you've made her so soft, Lord."

"She is soft," the Lord agreed,
"but I've also made her tough.
You have no idea what she can
endure or accomplish."

"Will she be able to think?" asked the angel.

The Lord replied, "Not only will she
be able to think, but she'll be able
to reason and negotiate, too."

The angel then noticed something, and reaching
out, touched the woman's cheek. "Oops, it looks
like you have a leak in this model. I told you that
you were trying to put too much into this one."

"That's not a leak," the Lord
corrected. "That's a tear."

"What's a tear for?" the angel asked.

The Lord said, "The tear is her way of
expressing her joy, her sorrow,
her pain, her disappointment, her love,
her loneliness, her grief, and her pride."

The angel was impressed.
"You are a genius, Lord. You thought of
everything! Woman is truly amazing."

"Yes, she is ... and all women will be.
All women will have strengths that amaze men.
They'll bear hardships and carry burdens; but
they'll hold happiness, love, and joy. They'll smile
when they want to scream. They'll sing when they
want to cry. They'll cry when they are happy and
laugh when they're nervous. They'll fight for
what they believe in. They'll stand up
to injustice. They won't take no for an answer
when they believe that there's a better solution.
They'll go without so their family can have.
They'll go to the doctor with a frightened friend.
They'll love unconditionally.

They'll cry when their children excel and cheer when their friends get awards. They'll be happy when they hear about a birth or a wedding. Their hearts will break when a friend dies. They'll grieve at the loss of a family member, yet they'll be strong when they think there's no strength left. They'll know that a hug and a kiss can heal a broken heart.

"Women will come in all shapes, sizes, and colours. They'll drive, fly, walk, or run to loved ones to show how much they care. Their hearts will make the world keep turning. They'll bring joy, hope and love. They'll have compassion and ideals. They'll give moral support to their family and friends. Woman will have vital things to say and everything to give.

"However, if there's one tiny flaw in women, it's that they will often forget their worth."

CHAPTER
12

GET
READY TO
FLY ...

♥

*"No matter how wonderful
this present moment is,
the future can be even more
fulfilling and joyous.
The universe always waits
in smiling response
for us to align our
thinking with its laws.
When we are in alignment,
everything flows.
It is possible.
You can do it.
I can do it.
We all can do it.
Make the effort.
You will be so pleased.
Your whole world
will change for the better."*

LOUISE HAY

*"If you can dream it,
you can do it.
Always remember this
whole thing was started
with a mouse"*

WALT DISNEY

Change is a gift.
It's moving us forwards,
always.

We all have wings,
but it is up
to us to have
the courage to fly.

With action,
anything in life
is possible ....